Spiders

Water Spiders

by Joanne Mattern

Consultant:
Pedro Barbosa, PhD
Department of Entomology
University of Maryland, College Park

CAPSTONE PRESS
a capstone imprint

First Facts is published by Capstone Press,
151 Good Counsel Drive, P.O. Box 669, Mankato, Minnesota 56002.
www.capstonepub.com

032010
005742LKF10

Books published by Capstone Press are manufactured with paper
containing at least 10 percent post-consumer waste.

Library of Congress Cataloging-in-Publication Data
Mattern, Joanne, 1963–
  Water spiders / by Joanne Mattern.
    p. cm.—(First facts. Spiders)
  Includes bibliographical references and index.
  Summary: "A brief introduction to water spiders, including their habitat, food, and
life cycle"—Provided by publisher.
  ISBN 978-1-4296-4522-5 (library binding)
  1. Water spider—Juvenile literature. I. Title. II. Series.
  QL458.42.A73M38 2011
  595.4'4—dc22

                            2010002258

Editorial Credits
Lori Shores, editor; Veronica Correia, designer; Eric Manske, production specialist

Photo Credits
Alamy/blickwinkel/Hartl, 7, 15; WILDLIFE GmbH, cover
Getty Images Inc./National Geographic/Robert F. Sisson, 16, 21;
    Photolibrary/Oxford Scientific, 13
Minden Pictures/Heidi & Hans-Juergen Koch, 5, 11, 20; Stephen Dalton, 8
Photolibrary/Oxford Scientific/Neil Bromhall, 19
Photoshot/Bruce Coleman/Wolfgang Bayer, 1

Essential content terms are **bold** and are defined at the bottom of the page
where they first appear.

Table of Contents

Super Swimmers

Water spiders make their homes underwater. They live in **freshwater** lakes and ponds. Water spiders are the only spiders that live underwater all the time. They use air bubbles to breathe underwater.

freshwater—water that has little or no salt

5

Spider Bodies

Most water spiders are less than 0.5 inch (13 millimeters) long. Like all spiders, these **arachnids** have two main body parts and eight legs. Their plump bodies are dark brown, red, or black.

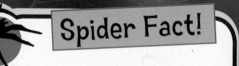

Spider Fact!

Unlike most other spiders, male water spiders are bigger than females.

arachnid—an animal with four pairs of legs and no backbone, wings, or antennae

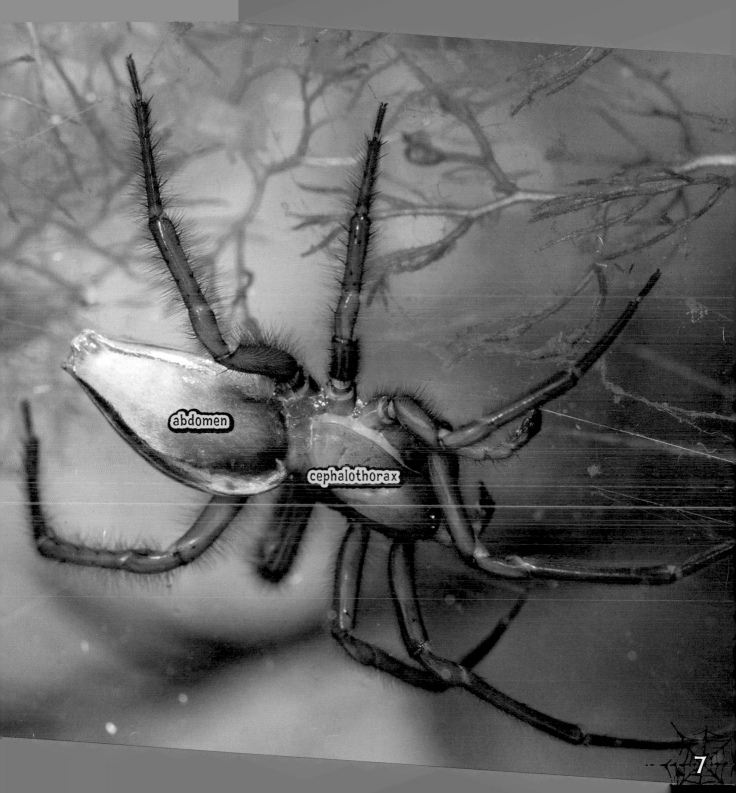

abdomen

cephalothorax

silk

Underwater Homes

Water spiders make small, bell-shaped webs with **silk**. They attach the webs to underwater plants. The spiders live inside the webs.

Spider Fact!

Water spiders are often called diving bell spiders.

silk—a string made by spiders

Home Wet Home

Water spiders live mainly in Great Britain and other parts of Europe. They are also found in parts of Asia and northern Africa.

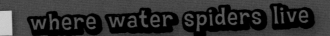

where water spiders live

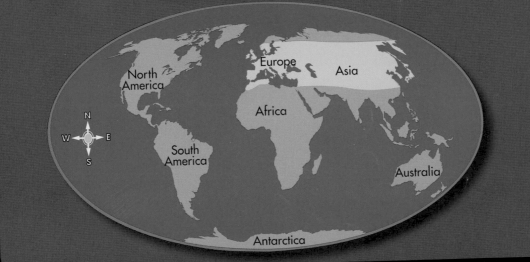

North America

Europe

Asia

Africa

South America

Australia

Antarctica

N
W E
S

Water spiders live in shallow lakes and ponds. They are sometimes found in streams and ditches filled with water.

On the Hunt

To hunt **prey**, water spiders sit in bubbles under their webs. The spider's legs dangle out of the bubble so it can swim out quickly. When an insect or tiny fish comes near, the spider grabs it.

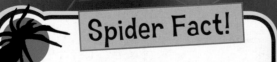

Spider Fact!

Water spiders return to their webs to eat their prey.

prey—an animal hunted by another animal for food

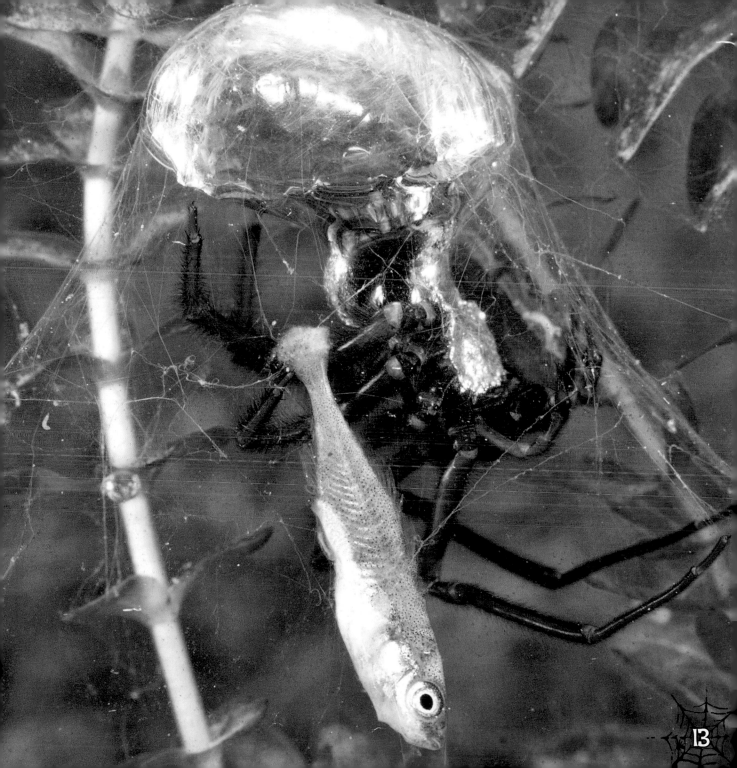

Deadly Bite

A water spider has two long, sharp **fangs**. These curved mouthparts are hollow like straws. Deadly **venom** flows through the fangs to kill prey.

Spider Fact!

Water spider venom is strong enough to kill small insects, fish, and crabs.

fang—a long, pointed toothlike mouthpart
venom—a harmful liquid produced by some animals

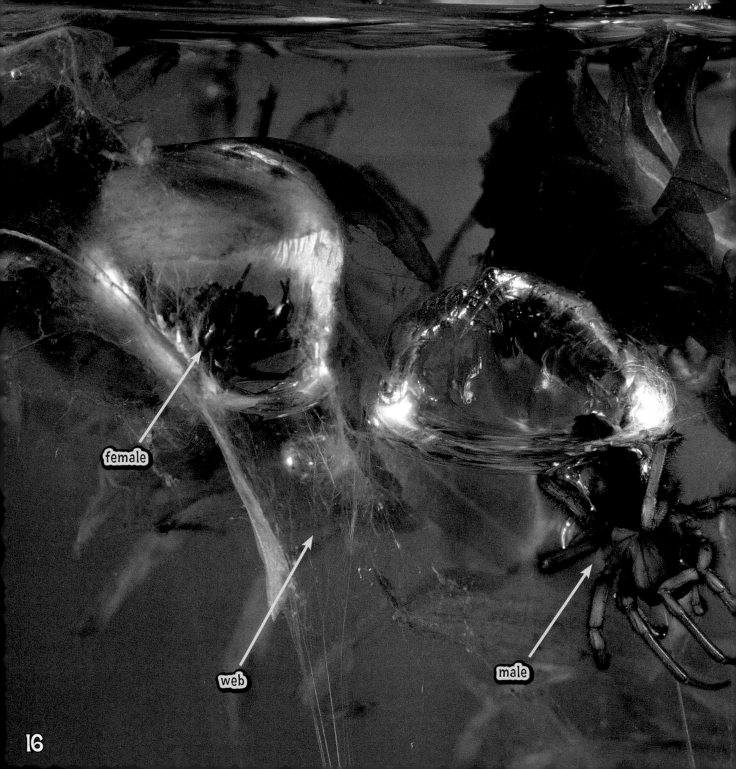

female

web

male

16

Family Matters

A male water spider searches for a female to **mate** with. When he finds one, he builds a new web near hers. The male spider connects the webs with a silk tube. When it's time to mate, he crawls through the tube and bites through the web wall.

mate—to join together to produce young

Baby Spiders

After mating, the female spider lays 30 to 70 eggs. She protects the eggs in an **egg sac**. After a few weeks, **spiderlings** chew through the egg sac. Then the spiderlings leave to live on their own.

Spider Fact!

Mother spiders carry egg sacs on their backs. They can also put them in air bubbles.

egg sac—a small pouch made of silk that holds spider eggs
spiderling—a young spider

Life Cycle of a Water Spider

Newborn

Spiderlings take care of themselves right away.

egg sac

Young

Some young water spiders live in empty snail shells.

Adult

Water spiders live about two years.

Sleepy Spiders

Water spiders **hibernate** in the winter. Some water spiders seal off their webs with silk and stay inside. Others spin webs inside empty shells. The spiders sleep inside until the water warms up.

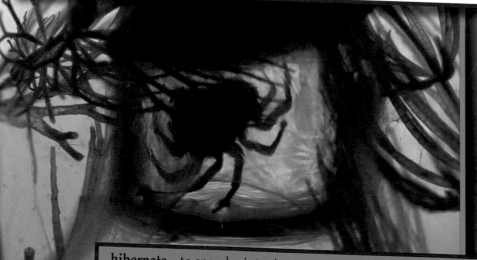

hibernate—to spend winter in a resting state as if in a deep sleep

Amazing but True!

Water spiders live underwater, but they still breathe air. These clever spiders store hundreds of air bubbles in their webs. They gather the bubbles at the surface of the water. Tiny leg hairs hold the bubbles while they swim to their webs.

Glossary

arachnid (uh-RACK-nid)—an animal with four pairs of legs and no backbone, wings, or antennae

egg sac (EG SAK)—a small pouch made of silk that holds spider eggs

fang (FANG)—a long, pointed toothlike mouthpart

freshwater (FRESH-wah-tuhr)—water that has little or no salt; most ponds, rivers, lakes, and streams have freshwater

hibernate (HYE-bur-nate)—to spend winter in a resting state as if in a deep sleep

mate (MATE)—to join together to produce young

prey (PRAY)—an animal hunted by another animal for food

silk (SILK)—a string made by spiders

spiderling (SPYE-dur-ling)—a young spider

venom (VEN-uhm)—a harmful liquid produced by some animals

Read More

Bishop, Nic. *Spiders.* New York: Scholastic Nonfiction, 2007.

Hartley, Karen, Chris Macro, and Philip Taylor. *Spider.* Bug Books. Chicago: Heinemann Library, 2008.

Woodward, John. *Spider.* Garden Minibeasts Up Close. New York: Chelsea Clubhouse, 2010.

Internet Sites

FactHound offers a safe, fun way to find Internet sites related to this book. All of the sites on FactHound have been researched by our staff.

Here's all you do:

Visit *www.facthound.com*

FactHound will fetch the best sites for you!

Index